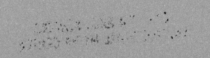

LEGENDS
OF
LANDFORMS

NATIVE AMERICAN LORE AND THE GEOLOGY OF THE LAND

Carole Garbuny Vogel

The Millbrook Press
Brookfield, Connecticut

Cover photograph courtesy of Tom Stack and Associates (© John Gerlach)
Photographs courtesy of Tom Stack and Associates: pp. 10 (© Terry Donnelly), 22 (© Brian Parker), 74
(© Milton Rand); FPG International: pp. 16 (© Gene Ahrens), 80; Oregon Historical Society: p. 28
(neg. #OrHi 40142); © National Geographic Society: pp. 34 (Richard H. Stewart), 56 (David S. Boyer), 62
(Robert F. Sisson); U. S. Geological Survey: p. 40 (Darton, N. H., 516); United States Department of the
Interior, National Park Service: pp. 46, 50 (Richard Frear), 68; National Geographic Image Collection: p. 86
(Chris Johns). Map by Michael Mills.

Library of Congress Cataloging-in-Publication Data
Vogel, Carole Garbuny
Legends of landforms: Native American lore and the geology of the land / Carole Garbuny Vogel.
p.   cm.
Summary: Presents the stories created by various native people to explain such natural wonders as the
Hot Springs of Arkansas, the Grand Canyon, Horseshoe Falls at Niagara Falls, and the Hawaiian Islands.
ISBN 0-7613-0272-7 (lib. bdg.)
1. Indians of North America—Folklore. 2. Landforms—United States—Folklore. 3. Human geography—
United States—Juvenile literature. 4. Legends—United States. [1. Landforms—Folklore.
2. Indians of North America—Folklore.] I. Title.
E98.F6V64   1999
398.2'089'97—dc21   98-30676   CIP   AC

Published by The Millbrook Press, Inc.
2 Old New Milford Road
Brookfield, Connecticut 06804

To my friend and great-grand aunt, Gisela Kohn Dollinger,

and in memory of her husband, Bernard Dollinger

This book was made possible, in part, by the assistance of the Anna Cross Giblin Nonfiction Work-in-Progress Grant given by the Society of Children's Book Writers and Illustrators.

ACKNOWLEDGMENTS

I would like to thank reference librarian Wikje Feteris, of Cary Memorial Library, Lexington, Massachusetts, for her help in tracking down obscure journals and out-of-print books that I never believed possible to find. Special thanks to Hayden Hirschfeld, a student at Harvard University, for his capable assistance with the myth research, and to Katy Z. Allen for her help at the inception of this project. I am grateful to my editor, Laura Walsh, for having the courage and wisdom to take on a book that meshed the mythical with the scientific. Where many editors said it couldn't be done, she saw the potential. And I would also like to thank the Society of Children's Book Writers and Illustrators, and James Giblin, for providing me with a work-in-progress grant. As always, I am extremely grateful to my writer friends, Florence Harris, Joyce A. Nettleton, Susan Sekuler, and my husband, Mark A. Vogel, for their excellent critiques and support. Finally, I am most indebted to the Native American storytellers who created, nurtured, and passed on the beautiful legends that I have adapted in this book.

INTRODUCTION

When astronauts aboard the space shuttle look down on Earth, they see a peaceful planet. Immense patches of white clouds swirl gracefully across blue oceans and brownish green continents. The oceans and landmasses appear tranquil. But the peaceful scene is merely an illusion.

Earth is a restless planet. Colliding continents, exploding volcanoes, earth-rattling quakes, colossal floods, as well as the action of ice, wind, running water, waves, and even the pull of gravity continually reshape Earth's surface. As a result nature sculpts spectacular landforms on the planet.

Anybody who has witnessed the full power of nature unleashed is unlikely to forget the experience. Long before the dawn of modern science, Native Americans witnessed some of the major geological and meteorological events that shaped the landscapes of North America. They interpreted these events according to their beliefs and preserved them as legends.

The ancients viewed the world as a blend of physical and spiritual parts. Mountains, rivers, lakes, the wind, moon, sun, and stars all were considered to be living beings with a spirit and personality of their own. Human beings, plants, and animals were linked together with the spirits inhabiting the earth and sky. Actions of individual humans or of whole tribes often resulted in dire consequences. Retribution for angering spirits frequently came in the form of earthquakes, floods, landslides, storms, and volcanic eruptions.

Legends of Landforms recounts the native legends of fearsome dragons, malevolent serpents, helpful giants, and other spirit beings, and how they relate to some of the most spectacular and unique landforms in North America. The book also provides a brief description of how scientists today understand the natural forces that formed these landscapes.

I decided to write *Legends of Landforms* while standing with my husband and two children in the middle of Highway 130 on the Big Island of Hawaii. A recent eruption of the flank of Kilauea Volcano had buried the road in front of us. From our vantage point we could see miles and miles of recently hardened lava. Shiny in places, the surface of the lava appeared to be a solid mass of black wrinkles, billows, and ropelike coils. Wisps of steam escaped from cracks throughout the area.

Awed by the sight, I told my children about Pele, the Hawaiian fire goddess, and how the Hawaiian people of long ago believed that Pele was responsible for volcanic eruptions. When I finished, my husband gave the children a scientific explanation for the volcanic activity. From my children's enthusiastic responses, I realized that understanding both scientific and sacred accounts of how the land came to be had contributed to their enjoyment and appreciation of this magnificent landscape much more than either account could have by itself. Now, what was left for me to do was to identify other spectacular land-forms, track down their legends, learn the science behind them, and help to show the reader new and unique ways to view the land around them. This book is a result of that effort.

Carole G. Vogel
Lexington, Massachusetts

CONTENTS

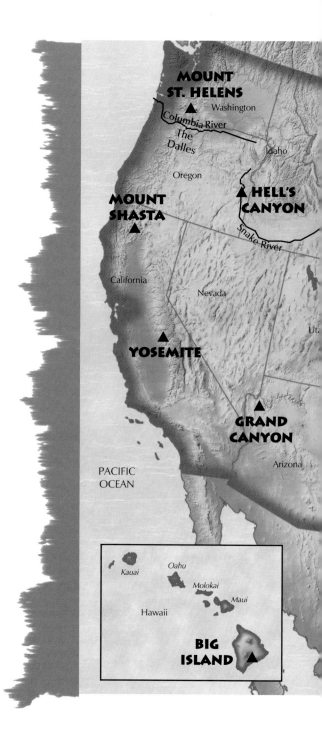

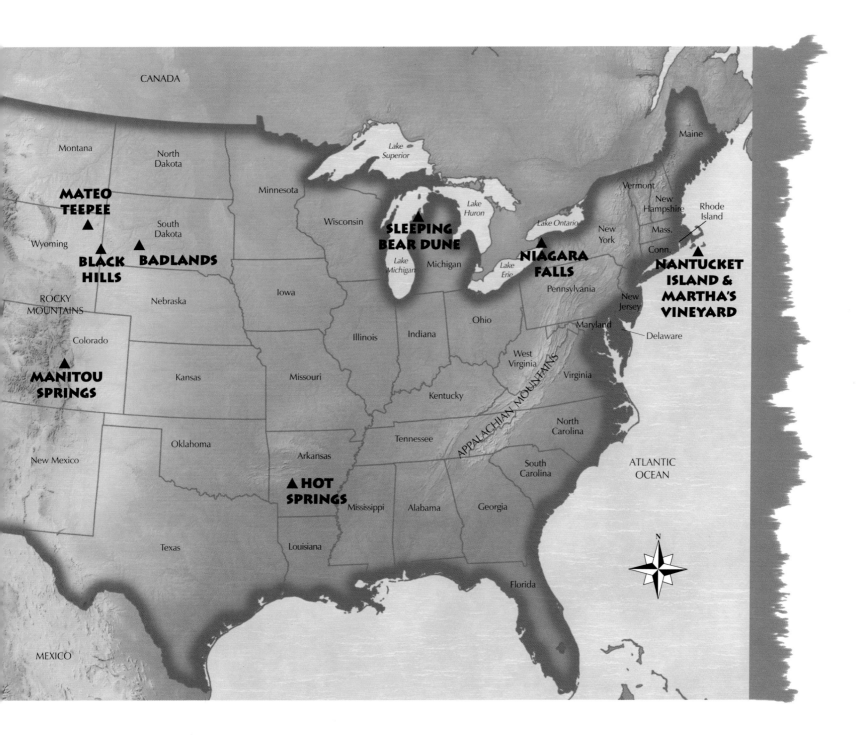

THE HOT SPRINGS OF ARKANSAS

OUACHITA MOUNTAINS, ARKANSAS

ADAPTED FROM TWO TUNICA LEGENDS

Long ago in the Valley of the Hot Springs, hot bubbly water rushed up from spring openings. Above the steep bluff where the springs emerged, clouds of steam billowed and drifted smokelike among lush green plants. For generations, the Tunicas and other tribes of the Caddo Nation found relief from arthritis, rheumatism, and other ailments in the soothing waters. Today, the hot springs still exist. However, all but three of the forty-seven spring openings have been covered.

In the beginning, when the sun had just learned its daily journey across the sky, the Kan-a-wag-as people roamed the Ouachita Mountains. The Great Spirit favored this tribe and provided for all its needs. He filled the forests with deer and wild turkey, the grasslands with bison and elk, and the fields with squash and maize. The people were content and they prospered. While the Great Spirit stood guard, no evil dared approach.

Many seasons passed and the Great Spirit faded from the thoughts of his people. The Great Spirit saw that he was forgotten and sadly turned his back on the tribes.

When Mogmothon, an evil dragon, saw that the people were out of favor with the Great Spirit, he came to live in the Ouachita Mountains. He made his home far below ground in a dark, bottomless cave. His eyes were like balls of liquid fire, so bright they blinded anyone who looked upon them. His claws were so powerful that not even the strongest of beasts could break free of his grasp. When he walked upon the land, his feet filled the valleys and storm clouds hid his head.

The dragon tormented the people. His heavy step shook the earth, toppling trees, triggering landslides, and leaving villages in ruin. His flaming breath set wildfires that scorched the crops and forced the wild animals to flee. In this time of terror, famine and disease spread.

The Kan-a-wag-as people, both young and old, began to die. Mogmothon satisfied his great hunger by feasting on the souls of the dead. From the burial grounds, the cries of grieving women and orphaned children rose in one long, mournful wail. The people feared they would soon all vanish from the earth.

They gathered in a great council of nations to search for the cause of their trouble. Soon they realized they had offended the Great Spirit, who had once been their protector. The people decided to make up for their sins. They began a period of prayer and fasting, meditation, and ceremonial dance. They pleaded for forgiveness.

Hearing the cries of his people, the Great Spirit returned to the Ouachita Mountains. He saw the devastated fields and wasted villages. He smelled the smoke from the burning forests and blackened grasslands. With love and pity, the Great Spirit looked upon his people and felt their agony. His feeling of compassion quickly changed to fury toward Mogmothon, the cause of this destruction.

The Great Spirit blotted out the sun and turned the air cold and thick. Then, with a deafening roar, he challenged the dragon. The Great Spirit called and called until the forests quivered and the mountains trembled.

Out of the cave stormed mighty Mogmothon. Fire and liquid rock spewed from his mouth and the ground beneath him rolled like ocean waves.

Earth, wind, and fire collided in a fearsome storm as Mogmothon and the Great Spirit struggled for dominion. For seven days the battle raged. The people cowered in their remaining homes, awed by the immense struggle taking place around them.

When it seemed that the earth could no longer withstand such violence, the Great Spirit tore a handful of stars from the sky and flung them at Mogmothon. The stars, colder than the coldest winter night, numbed the dragon's arms and froze his evil breath. They turned his eyes of fire into sightless balls of ice. They froze his blood and weakened his legs. Mogmothon fell to the ground.

The Great Spirit lifted the fallen dragon. As the people watched, he threw the evil creature into the bottomless cave and sealed the entrance with a mountain.

Under a clear sky, the Great Spirit returned to the place where the wounded dragon had fallen. There he opened the earth. From the gap, pure spring waters poured forth as his eternal gift of life and health to the people.

To this day, defeated and powerless, Mogmothon lies trapped beneath the mountain. Warm healing waters bubble out from the ground in the spot where he fell. We call these waters the Hot Springs of Arkansas.

The waters of the hot springs originate from rainwater that falls in the Hot Springs valley, and on the ridges flanking the valley. The rainwater first seeps through a layer of shallow, rocky soil. Then it passes through hard and brittle rock that is perforated with cracks and tiny pores. As it descends, the water picks up some minerals from the surrounding rocks. The temperature of rocks beneath the earth's crust increases with depth. Apparently this natural increase in temperature is sufficient to heat the water.

The water travels downward at a rate of a mere foot or so a year. It takes about 4,000 years for the water to reach a maximum depth of 6,000 to 8,000 feet. But the return trip is much faster. The heated water rises relatively rapidly to the surface through a zone of fractured rock—a journey that takes about a year. More than 1,000,000 gallons of water with an average temperature of 143°F gush from the springs each day.

The Valley of the Hot Springs is located on the eastern edge of the Ouachita Mountains in Arkansas. Once the valley was narrow, with a creek running along its floor. Springs on the steep hillside east of the creek spewed out hot water, which then cascaded into the creek. Over the centuries, the flowing hot water deposited a thick blanket of calcium minerals on the hillside. Here and there, thickets of green plants dotted the landscape. The minerals no longer form on the hillside because most of the hot water has been deliberately diverted.

Like the native people, the European settlers recognized the healing properties of the hot springs. Men and women suffering from rheumatism and other ailments sought relief in the steaming spring water. In 1832, the federal government claimed the springs and the land around them for public use. At first, the bathing facilities for the new Americans were just the natural shallow pools. However, by the late 1830s the first bathhouses—little more than huts—were built along Hot Springs Creek.

Soon more elaborate bathhouses were constructed and the water was diverted to them through wooden troughs. But the valley was too narrow to accommodate larger bathhouses. So in 1883 Hot Springs Creek was covered over by a stone arch, which did not impede the normal flow. Rock and dirt were placed on the top and sides of the arch. This raised the valley floor by 20 feet, making it broad and flat enough to support large buildings. A few of the springs were covered and their water was diverted through pipes to new, larger bathing facilities.

In 1921 the hot springs area was declared a national park. Development continued well into recent times. Now all but three of the 47 hot springs have been covered. The water from the covered springs is piped to a central reservoir and then channeled to the bathhouses.

The Valley of the Hot Springs would be unrecognizable to the native people who enjoyed it long ago. Even present-day visitors often ask, "Where are the hot springs?"

THE
GRAND CANYON

NORTHWESTERN ARIZONA

AN UTE LEGEND

The Grand Canyon in northwestern Arizona is a mind-boggling gash in the earth's surface. It is about 277 miles long, as much as 18 miles wide, and in some places about a mile deep. Acclaimed not only for its immense size, the Grand Canyon is also admired for its unusual rock formations and its beautiful array of colors. The rock that makes up the canyon is primarily red, but it has striking hues of cream, gray, green, pink, brown, black, and violet. The deepest and most spectacular part of the canyon lies in Grand Canyon National Park.

Long ago when spirits still spoke to human beings, there lived in the Southwest a tribe led by a great and wise chief. The people loved their chief and looked to him for guidance in all matters. His wife was a beautiful woman, beloved in her own right for her many acts of kindness.

The chief and his wife led full and happy lives until one day the wife became ill. Helplessly, the chief watched as life ebbed from her. No medicines or prayers could prevent her death. When she breathed no more, the chief held a funeral ceremony and sadly buried her. Afterward, loneliness consumed him, and no one could comfort him. Day and night the chief grieved, and he wandered the desert in despair.

His people, saddened by their own loss and by their leader's anguish, mourned too. Their sorrow grew and they neglected their crops, put aside their weaving, and ignored their feast days. No singing or dancing enlivened the village. Children clung to their mothers, and even the dogs lay listless in the shadows. Lost in grief, the chief could not see the pain of his people.

Concerned, the Great Spirit sent his messenger, Ta-voats, to comfort the chief. Ta-voats told the chief that his wife dwelt in a happier land. And he promised that once the chief's work among his people was done, he could join his wife there. But the chief was not persuaded. He needed to see for himself where his dead wife had gone. So Ta-voats offered to take the chief to his wife but only on one condition: the chief would no longer mourn his beloved upon his return. The chief agreed.

A forbidding landscape of high mesas and rugged mountains separated the land of the living from the home of the dead. No living being had ever succeeded in crossing this barrier. Ta-voats took his mystical sphere—an immense ball of fire—and began to roll it across the forbidden land. As it rolled, the ball cleaved the ground. Blazing through solid rock, it forged an immense, deep trail, which grew ever more narrow as it reached the bottom.

The chief and Ta-voats followed the fiery sphere into the land of the dead. There the chief saw the blessings the Great Spirit had bestowed upon the souls of the departed. In this beautiful land, the streams teemed with fish, and the forests abounded with game. A basket filled with pine nuts always remained full no matter how many nuts were taken. A bottle of cactus wine never emptied although many souls took refreshment from it. The chief observed that in this land there was no pain or hunger, no want or sorrow. Only joy and happiness prevailed. Finally, in the distance he beheld his wife, who smiled and waved at him. He saw that she was happy.

Suddenly, the veil of grief lifted from him, and a vision of his tribe appeared. For the first time, he became aware of the pain and misery of his people. He realized they needed his guidance to survive. Ready to rejoin the living, the chief returned to his tribe with Ta-voats.

As Ta-voats was about to say farewell, he admonished the chief, "Never walk this trail again during life. Warn your people not to go this way."

Although the chief agreed, Ta-voats worried that the people would try to travel to the land of the departed once they learned of its pleasures. So Ta-voats rolled a river onto the trail—a wild, raging river that covered the path completely. Today we know this river as the Colorado, flowing through the magnificent gorge we call the Grand Canyon.

If you looked closely at the walls of the Grand Canyon you would see that they consist of different layers of rock. Geologists can "read" these rock layers like a book to learn about the canyon's history. Each separate layer formed during a different period in the canyon's life. The oldest rock can be seen along the bottom of the canyon and the youngest rock can be seen at the top.

The Grand Canyon's story began more than 2 billion years ago when the earth was half as old as it is now and active volcanoes dotted much of what is now America's West. A huge, shallow sea covered the area where the canyon now lies. Sediments—particles of silt, sand, and clay in the seawater—drifted slowly to the seafloor. Over millions of years these sediments, along with lava flows from the volcanoes, collected in layers. As each new layer was added, the one beneath it hardened into rock as a result of the increased pressure.

Eventually, forces deep inside the earth buckled the rock layers and pushed them into mountains as high as the Rocky Mountains stand today. Over time the forces of erosion—wind, water, ice, and gravity—wore these mountains down. The sea invaded again and a second mountain range emerged and wore away.

About 65 million years ago, around the time when the dinosaurs disappeared from Earth, the land rose once more. This time it formed a plateau, a large area of flat land that towers above the surrounding land. The Colorado River flowed over the plateau and gradually cut through its rock layers to create the Grand Canyon. This process took millions of years and still continues today.

THE SWEET AND BITTER SPRINGS

MANITOU SPRINGS, COLORADO

AN UTE LEGEND

Cradled in a valley on the eastern slope of Pikes Peak in Colorado lies a labyrinth of more than two dozen mineral springs. These springs are held sacred by the Ute people, who named them Manitou Springs in honor of the Great Spirit. Like the Hot Springs of Arkansas, the Manitou Springs were later covered and even paved over. Today, however, many of the previously capped springs are hooked up to spigots or fountains to allow people easier access to the water.

Hundreds of winters ago, in a time when all tribes lived in peace, two thirsty hunters met at a tiny stream. One hunter was Shoshone and a stranger to the area. The other, who lived nearby, was Comanche. The Shoshone carried a large deer on his back. He dropped the carcass on the ground and expressed his thanks to the Great Spirit for his success in the hunt and for the refreshing water he was about to drink.

The Comanche, unsuccessful after a long day's hunt, felt quite irritable. He was not only jealous of the stranger's bounty, but he was also angry with himself for failing to give an offering to the Great Spirit. He dipped his face in the stream to quench his thirst. When he looked up, he saw the Shoshone drinking from the source of the stream—a spring that bubbled up from the rocks.

An evil spirit took over the Comanche, making him quarrelsome. "Why does a stranger drink at the spring," he demanded, "when one to whom it belongs is satisfied with the water that runs from it?"

"I may drink here," replied the Shoshone calmly, "because the Great Spirit, Manitou, gave the spring to all his children so they may drink the water pure at its source. Water that runs over the ground is for the animals. I am Ausaqua, a leader of the Shoshone nation. I drink at the source."

"The Shoshone are merely a tribe of the Comanche," declared the agitated man. "I am Wacomish, one of the leaders of the Comanche. Why do you dare to drink above me?"

"The Great Spirit said the Comanche and the Shoshone are brothers," replied Ausaqua. "The spring belongs to both nations."

"I am the leader of the Shoshone, just as I am the leader of my own people," said Wacomish. "You will do as I command."

"No," said Ausaqua. "When Manitou made his children, whether Shoshone or Comanche, Arapaho, Cheyenne, or Paiute, he gave them the pure water of the spring to quench their thirst. He did not say to one, 'Drink here,' and to another, 'Drink there!' He gave the spring to *all* who are thirsty." With these words, Ausaqua stooped down to drink once again.

Enraged, Wacomish pounced on the kneeling hunter and forced his head under the water. He held it there until the Shoshone drowned.

As the Comanche stood over the dead man, horror and remorse suddenly replaced the rage in his heart. He dragged the body away from the water. As he did, bubbles gurgled up from the bottom of the spring and hissed as they met the air. A thin cloud arose from the water, and slowly the figure of an ancient man emerged. The Comanche murderer knew this spirit was Wankanaga, the father of both the Comanche and the Shoshone tribes, and he began to tremble.

"Today," said Wankanaga to the quavering man, "you have severed the bond between two of the greatest nations on Earth. The blood of the Shoshone hunter cries out for vengeance." With that, the spirit took a club and struck the Comanche dead. The body fell into the spring, turning the water bitter and putrid.

In memory of the noble Shoshone hunter who came in peace, Wankanaga struck a nearby rock with the same club. The rock opened into a round basin, and clear, sweet water instantly gushed from it. This spring, known as the Manitou Spring, has quenched the thirst of many a hunter ever since. The bitter spring was called the Sulfur Spring. To this day, its water is so foul that not even a person half-dead from thirst could drink from it. Both springs endure near each other as a reminder of the terrible murder of the brave Shoshone and the swift justice of Wankanaga.

The formation of Manitou Springs began about 75 million years ago. At that time, the same shallow sea that covered the Grand Canyon region also covered what is now the Rocky Mountains. For millions of years sediments collected in layers on the seafloor and gradually hardened into limestone and other kinds of sedimentary rock. Then 65 million years ago, at the same time that uplift formed the Grand Canyon region, mountain building began in earnest in the Rockies.

Billion-year-old granite rock lay beneath the sedimentary rock. Under pressure, the granite began to soften and expand, like toothpaste being squeezed out of a narrow tube. The granite rose and bent the overlying sedimentary rock into an arch. Gradually, erosion wore away this arched rock. But the granite had also spread sideways, covering surrounding sedimentary rock and protecting it from the forces of erosion.

The uplift continued and the ranges of the southern Rockies grew higher and higher. Eventually more than fifty-three peaks, including Pikes Peak, rose to elevations greater than

14,000 feet. All this uplift created majestic, rugged mountains. It also sliced the region with faults—large cracks in the rocks—that still exist today. Chief among the faults close to Pikes Pike is the Ute Pass Fault.

Near the Ute Pass Fault, underground water rises through cracked limestone. As it moves upward, the water absorbs carbon dioxide from the limestone. The carbon dioxide becomes part of the water just as carbon dioxide is part of soda pop.

Far below the surface, the water is under pressure, which keeps the carbon dioxide dissolved in the water. But as the water gushes upward, the pressure decreases. When the water reaches the surface, the carbon dioxide bubbles out, giving the Manitou Springs water a slight fizz.

Like the water that flows from the Hot Springs of Arkansas, the Manitou Springs water comes from rain and snowmelt that seeped below the surface. However, the water at Manitou Springs does not migrate as far underground, so it is not heated.

Each of the springs at Manitou Springs rises through a different channel, picking up different minerals along the way. The minerals give the water a distinctive taste. The sweet spring referred to in the legend is still considered the best tasting of all the springs. It is known today as Manitou Spring or Soda Spring. The bitter spring is called either Sulfur Spring or Shoshone Spring. Its bitter taste probably comes from the high concentration of sulfur in the water.

HELL'S CANYON

BORDER OF IDAHO AND OREGON

A NEZ PERCÉ LEGEND

Hell's Canyon on the Snake River is the deepest gorge in North America, and possibly the deepest gorge on Earth. You could stack fourteen Washington Monuments on top of each other inside the gorge, with room left over. At its deepest point Hell's Canyon plunges down 7,900 feet—nearly a mile and a half—eclipsing the Grand Canyon in depth by more than 2,000 feet. The gorge is 125 miles long, and it averages a mere 10 miles in width, rim to rim. Hell's Canyon forms part of the boundary between Idaho and Oregon. On the Idaho side, the Seven Devils Mountains loom above the canyon. The Blue Mountains rise up to the west in Oregon.

In the days long gone, seven cruel giants dwelt in the Blue Mountains in what is now eastern Oregon. Once each year, the giants crossed the Snake River and stalked the land to the east of their home. They raided villages and devoured all the young children they could find. Terrified mothers fled with their small ones and tried to hide them. But the giants still found many of the children.

No man was tall enough or strong enough to fight the seven giants. Not even all of the men fighting together could defeat them. The people feared that soon no children would be left. Finally the chief decided to seek the help of Coyote, a spirit being with mystical powers.

Coyote had battled giants and other tyrants before, but he had never fought seven giants at one time. So Coyote sought the advice of his good friend, Fox.

"We should dig seven very deep holes across the giants' usual path near the Snake River," suggested Fox. "Then we will fill the holes with a boiling reddish liquid."

Coyote summoned all the digging animals—the woodchucks, the badgers, the foxes, the moles—even the rats, mice, and chipmunks—to assist with the digging. When the holes were finished, Coyote filled each one with a reddish boiling liquid.

When the time came for their annual plunder, the seven giants marched down the path with their heads held high, confident that nothing could stop them. Suddenly the giants stumbled into the holes and sank into the hot liquid. They struggled to escape but the holes were too deep. The giants succeeded only in splattering the hot liquid a day's journey in every direction.

Then Coyote stepped out of his hiding place. "I am punishing you for your wickedness," he announced. "I will turn you into seven high mountains as a reminder that punishment follows wrongdoing."

That said, Coyote caused the giants to grow taller. Then he transformed them into the mountain peaks known today as the Seven Devils Mountains. To prevent others of the giants' family from crossing into the land, Coyote struck the earth hard. A deep gash opened up at the foot of the new peaks. Thus, Hell's Canyon was born.

And the red hot liquid? It flowed into the cracks in the ground and hardened. It became copper, which is mined in the region to this very day.

The Snake River roars through Hell's Canyon. This powerful, fast-moving river, with numerous rapids, carries nearly twice as much water as the Colorado River, which carved the Grand Canyon. In the inner gorge of Hell's Canyon, black cliffs rise almost straight up for thousands of feet above the river channel. Often no more than 200 feet separate the opposing walls of the canyon. It would be easy to believe that the Snake River carved out Hell's Canyon, but it did not.

The story of Hell's Canyon begins about 17 million years ago—a mere blink in geologic time. Back then, gently rolling hills and valleys covered the territory where the gorge now lies. To the north lay the Columbia River. Just to the south, the Snake River flowed peacefully on its journey to the Pacific. It emptied into the ocean somewhere along what is now the California coast.

Then great fissures ripped open the earth's crust in the land between the Cascade Mountains and the Rocky Mountains. Huge amounts of lava surged up through these cracks and spilled out in all directions. In just a few days, the lava traveled great distances before cooling and hardening. So much lava spewed out that it covered much of the terrain in a layer of black basaltic rock.

Thousands of years later another torrent of lava poured out of the fissures and buried the first layer. More lava followed every 13,000 years or so, building up the land. The thickness of the individual lava layers ranged from 10 to 200 feet. Over a period of 5 million years, the layers formed a high, flat landscape known as the Columbia Plateau. The plateau had an average thickness of about 6,000 feet and covered parts of the states of Washington, Oregon, and Idaho, including the Hell's Canyon region. However, the ancient Snake River remained untouched.

Meanwhile, far below the surface of the Hell's Canyon region new stresses took hold. Earthquakes rattled the land and pushed up the southeast corner of the Columbia Plateau. The uplift continued and this corner of the plateau began to crack. Enormous blocks of rock slowly emerged through the fractured plateau. Over millions of years, these blocks became the Seven Devils Mountains and Wallowa Mountains.

Further south, the Owyhee Mountains slowly formed and blocked the path of the Snake River. Cut off from its route to the sea and with nowhere else to go, the water pooled behind the mountain barrier. Gradually enough water collected to form a huge lake.

About a million years ago, a small new river began to flow on the opposite side of the mountain barrier. This river found a series of weak spots—deep cracks in the rocks—beneath the mountain. The new river tunneled downward through the cracks, enlarging them as it progressed. Finally the river eroded the rocks in the part of the mountain that separated the river from the impounded lake. Like a gigantic bathtub coming unplugged, the lake began to drain into the newer river. Then suddenly, the tremendous force of the water burst through the already weakened rocks, unleashing a flood of titanic proportions.

The towering mass of water gouged a steep and narrow channel through the underlying rocks, sculpting the majestic cliffs visible in Hell's Canyon today. The flood may have lasted only a day or two but its impact still lingers on. When the rampage was over, the lake was gone, and Hell's Canyon had been carved. The Snake River now flowed in its new channel along the canyon bottom and joined up with the Columbia. Once more it had found its way to the sea.

The first humans to inhabit the canyon arrived millions of years after the flood. They probably lived there about 15,000 years ago and left few traces. The earliest Euro-American explorers found two major tribes living in the canyon. At the southern end dwelt the Western Shoshone and at the northern end, the Nez Percé. The two tribes were not on friendly terms and the Nez Percé claimed most of the canyon. Skirmishes between the two tribes frequently took place in the canyon.

THE
BLACK HILLS

SOUTHWESTERN SOUTH DAKOTA
AND EASTERN WYOMING

A LAKOTA SIOUX LEGEND

The Black Hills are small, isolated mountains, located east of the Rocky
Mountains in southwestern South Dakota and eastern Wyoming.
Along the southwestern edge of the Black Hills is a valley surrounded by
steep, jagged cliffs. Red sandstone topped with white rock makes up the
valley's northern walls and gives the valley its name—Red Canyon.
According to Lakota tradition, Red Canyon is part of a racetrack that was
once the site of the most fantastic race of all time. The other part of the track
lies within a row of ledgelike rises that encircle the Black Hills.

L ong ago when the world was young, a prairie covered the land where the Black Hills now stand. There the grass grew so thick that it rippled in the wind like waves on a sea. This fertile land was inhabited by human beings, but they were not alone. Four-legged creatures, larger than any animal now living, prowled the land. They feasted on humans and any animals unfortunate enough to cross their paths.

And if this were not enough, giant mosquitoes the size of eagles thronged the skies. With long stingers as sharp as new tomahawks, the mosquitoes stunned their prey and sucked out the blood. Unlike the mosquitoes of today, these insects were not satisfied with just a taste of human blood, they wanted all of it. When the mosquitoes finished with a victim, all that remained was an empty, lifeless vessel.

One day it occurred to the people to bring order to this chaos. So they called representatives of all the animals together for a meeting. There it was decided that a race would be held to test the endurance and stamina of every kind of creature, including humans. The results of the race would determine the proper place in the world for each animal class. The race would decide which animals would be the hunters and which would be the prey.

Messengers chosen from the fastest animals scattered in the directions of the winds to announce the race. Strict rules were established to assure that the contest was fair and that even the smallest and weakest animals would have a fighting chance. The penalty for breaking any of the rules was death. The runners were to race without stopping while the sun rose and set one hundred times. Pausing even for food and water would be risky.

Meanwhile, a search committee scouted the countryside for a suitable site to lay out a circular racetrack. The track needed to be long enough and wide enough to accommodate all the animals who wanted to participate in the race. After much searching, the committee decided to build the racetrack on the prairie.

On the day of the race, animals of all varieties, shapes, sizes, and colors arrived to compete. A voice announced with the sound of thunder, "Your fate is at hand."

Immediately the multitude of animals took off in a giant stampede and sped around the track. The earth trembled beneath the impact of their feet. Clouds of dust billowed high in the air, choking the flocks of birds that circled above the animals on the track.

Before the sun set on the first day, the screams and moans of the weaker animals rose above the din as they were trampled beneath the pounding feet of the stronger animals. Occasionally a bird would shriek and drop to the ground as a result of exhaustion or a collision with another bird.

The race went on and on. Faster runners zoomed past slower ones; exhausted ones dropped out. The remaining contestants developed a wild, pulsating stomp that churned the earth and thrashed the air. Crazed from hunger and fatigue, the runners shouted insanely, adding to the frenzy.

This spectacle displeased the Great Spirit and he decided to put a swift end to it. In the center of the racetrack, he caused the land to bulge. A small mound appeared and instantly grew bigger. As the ground shuddered and groaned, the mound rose higher and faster. Lightning crackled in the air.

Suddenly, with an indescribable clamor, the mound burst apart, belching out fire and rocks. Smoke and ash shot skyward. Molten rock and hot ash poured down upon the runners, killing them all.

Soon the air cleared and an eerie quiet replaced the tumult. Inside the circle of dead runners an immense pile of broken rocks towered majestically above the rubble. The Lakota call these rocks *Paha Sapa*, the Black Hills.

Because the animals never finished the race, no winner was declared. According to legend, however, the lowly magpie led the birds. And the *unkche ghila*, a gargantuan animal larger than any alive today, overtook all the ground animals.

The Black Hills loom about 3,000 feet above the surrounding high plain. The Sioux named the range the *Black Hills* because thick pine forests covering the slopes gave the mountains a dark appearance when viewed from afar.

Millions of years ago the Black Hills were high mountains formed by the same kind of uplift of ancient rock that created the Rocky Mountains. Over time, the forces of erosion whittled down the lofty mountain peaks, carving out the rugged rock formations seen in the Black Hills today. The region is known for its deep canyons and rocky hills.

The ancient Sioux occasionally found the fossilized bones of large extinct animals in the Badlands adjoining the Black Hills. They understood that giant creatures once roamed the land but were now extinct.

The Black Hills are sacred to the Sioux, and a treaty with the Federal Government, signed in 1868, guaranteed their rights to the land. However, in 1874 gold was discovered in the Black Hills and thousands of white miners and fortune seekers poured into the territory. When the Sioux tried to defend their land, General George Custer led the U.S. Cavalry in a counter-attack. The Sioux succeeded in stopping Custer and his men at the battle of the Little Bighorn. Custer and more than 200 soldiers died there. However, the Sioux victory was short-lived, and by 1877 they were forced to relinquish their rights to the land. The Lakota people belong to the Sioux nation.

THE BADLANDS

SOUTH DAKOTA

A YANKTON SIOUX LEGEND

To the east of the Black Hills lies a land of steep cliffs, deep gullies, and jagged spires. The region is so devoid of plant life and so difficult to traverse that it goes by the name of the Badlands. Here temperatures range from −39°F in winter to 112°F in summer. Little precipitation falls during the year, but when it does it often comes in the form of pounding rain or blinding blizzards. Fossilized remains of giant rhinoceros, saber-toothed tigers, three-toed horses, and other extinct species have been found in the sedimentary rocks of the Badlands. As these animals could not have survived the harsh conditions of the Badlands today, they are proof that the region's climate was once much more temperate and able to support a great diversity of plants and animals.

Long ago, so far in the past that you cannot measure it, a high plain lay to the east of the Black Hills. Grass, trees, and wildflowers covered the plain. Streams flush with fish and turtles flowed through it. But most importantly, the plain abounded with buffalo, deer, and elk.

Each year when the autumn wind blew with the breath of frost and painted the leaves red, orange, and yellow, many Sioux tribes came to this rich land. The plain was their sacred hunting ground. And autumn was the time of the great hunt, when the men killed enough game to supply their families with food for the winter.

The Great Spirit declared that the hunting ground was neutral territory. Tribes that warred with each other in other seasons called a truce when they met there. Quarrels were not permitted.

For many snows the Sioux kept the peace among themselves. The weaker tribes had no reason to fear the stronger ones. Even enemies who clashed during spring and summer sang, danced, and competed in friendly games with one another.

Then one day a fierce tribe from the western mountains discovered the rich plain. They came from a land with few deer, elk, and buffalo. The intruders saw the bounty of the plain and claimed it for themselves. Blind to the peace and friendship fostered in the land, the trespassers killed the best game and refused to allow the Sioux to set up camp. In no time at all, they drove all the Sioux from the plain.

The Sioux fought bravely to retake their ancient hunting ground. Without the game it provided, many families would starve during the cold winter months. Courageous as they were, however, the Sioux could not defeat their enemy. The intruders' aim with bow and arrow was unerring. Again and again the hostile mountain men crushed the Sioux in battle. Many brave men perished, and the women mourned the loss of their husbands, sons, and fathers.

Finally the elders called a great council of all the Sioux tribes. The people fasted for many days and held ceremonial dances to appease the spirits. The shamans offered prayers, and some people afflicted themselves with agonizing tortures to gain the spirits' favor. But the spirits gave no sign that they had heard the pleas, and the people despaired.

Then, at long last the people received their answer. The midday sky darkened as though it belonged to the blackest of nights. Streaks of lightning slashed the air, and thunder roared and shook the ground. Then strange fires broke out all over the plain, lighting up the countryside with an eerie glow.

Beneath the plain the earth quivered. The land rolled up and down like waves in a great, stormy sea. Suddenly the ground opened up and swallowed the barbarous intruders. With them went their teepees and all the grass, trees, streams, rivers, and animals.

Terrified, the Sioux watched from a great distance. But just as abruptly as the tumult had started, it ended. The fires flickered out and the ground stopped rolling. But with the return of daylight, the Sioux saw that the fertile land had been changed into hard, barren rock. What was once a beautiful plain now was desolate wasteland.

The Great Spirit had punished the people he had spared. He had destroyed the land that had caused so much strife among his children. To this day the Badlands remain in this wretched state as a reminder of his wrath.

One hundred million years ago, the same shallow sea that once covered the Rocky Mountain and Grand Canyon regions also covered the area where the Badlands now stand. About 65 million years ago, when upheaval thrust up the Rocky Mountains and the Black Hills it also raised the land beneath the shallow sea. The water drained away, leaving behind the muddy seabed.

The sediments at the bottom of the seabed formed a layer of dark shale about 2,000 feet thick. Within the shale are fossils of extinct creatures that swam in the ancient sea. About 40 million years ago, water carrying sand and gravel washed down from the Black Hills onto the shale. A marshy plain began to form.

Wind carried ash that had been ejected from volcanoes in the west and deposited it on the marshy plain. Sediments continued to wash down from the mountains. As new layers of ash and sediment were added, the underlying ones gradually hardened into rock. The layers varied in thickness and hardness. This went on for about 11 million years, building up the plain to an elevation as high as 5,500 feet above sea level.

During this time, an abundance of plants and animals thrived on the warm, marshy plain. It was in this prehistoric wilderness that giant rhinoceros, saber-toothed tigers, and three-toed horses made their home. The remains of some of these plants and animals fell into the sediments. As the sediments turned into stone, the remains turned into fossils.

The climate turned colder and drier. Hardier grasses replaced the marsh plants, and animals better suited to the harsher climate replaced the marsh-dwelling animals. Now the soil became too dry to support a luxuriant plant cover that would protect it from the elements. When rain did come, it pounded into the ground, chiseling away at the rocks. Wind, ice, and running water also contributed to the weathering and erosion of the rocks. Different kinds of rocks wore away at different rates and in different patterns. This difference in weathering led to the unusual variation in the landscape.

MATEO TEEPEE

WYOMING

A CHEYENNE LEGEND

High above the grassy plains and pine forests of northeastern Wyoming looms a monstrous shaft of bare rock. Long vertical ridges scour this huge stumplike formation. It appears so out of place that it has sparked the imagination of many people. Hollywood filmmakers used it as the landing site for aliens in Close Encounters of the Third Kind. Some native tribes call this formation Mateo Teepee, *meaning* "Grizzly Bear Lodge." They object strenuously to the white explorers' disrespectful name for it: "Devil's Tower."

A band of people once camped in the rugged, pine-studded hills of what is now Wyoming. Near a stream, the families pitched their tepees close together in a tight circle. No one knew what hostile tribes or ferocious beasts might be lurking in the wilderness. So the fathers and the mothers warned their children to stay close to camp until scouts searched the countryside and determined the dangers.

However, as the men hunted and the women prepared the noon meal, seven young maidens wandered away. The girls meant to obey, but the day was so pleasant and the countryside so beautiful they forgot the warnings. The maidens pranced and played in the sunlight. They picked flowers and somersaulted in the grass. The girls roamed so far away that the smoke from their tribe's campfires became a distant haze on the horizon.

Seemingly out of nowhere a pack of ferocious grizzly bears came upon them. Terrified, the maidens raced back toward the camp. Growling and gnashing their teeth, the bears gave chase and easily closed the gap. Just as the grizzlies were about to pounce, the girls leaped onto a rock. Shaking with fright, they prayed to the spirits to save them.

Immediately the rock began to grow upward, lifting the girls away from the bears. Higher and higher it stretched as the angry bears jumped and clawed at its sides. Sharp pieces of rock broke off the rising tower and rained down upon the frustrated beasts. Again and again the bears tried to reach the girls. But the sides were too smooth and too steep. Try as they might, the bears could not reach the top.

The bears finally gave up and headed down the column. They were so tired, they slipped, crashed to the ground, and were killed by the rocks at the column's base.

Peering down from the top of the column, the girls saw the grizzlies fall. Anxiously they scrutinized the battered bodies, looking for signs of movement. When they saw none, the maidens gathered together the flowers they had picked, and braided them into a long rope. They anchored the rope to the top of the rock. Then one by one they scrambled down the rope until all seven girls reached the ground.

The bodies of the bears have long vanished. Their claw marks, however, can still be observed on the side of Mateo Teepee.

The origin of Mateo Teepee is not as mysterious as its appearance suggests. It is merely the remains of a would-be volcano. Mateo Teepee started to form around the time the Rocky Mountains did. From deep within the earth molten rock welled up through the crust but cooled before breaking through to the surface. The magma solidified in a rock mass many miles long, but just a few thousand feet beneath the surface. Before the magma totally cooled, long blobs pushed upward through cracks in the overlying rock. One of these blobs was particularly large. As it hardened, the rock cracked into a series of vertical columns, just as mud cracks and shrinks as it dries. This created large columns around the sides of the new rock formation.

Layers of softer rock covered the formation completely. Gradually wind, rain, ice, and the flowing water of a neighboring river stripped away the softer rock. Ultimately, these processes exposed the harder rock that forms Mateo Teepee. Erosive forces continue to eat away at the rugged formation. Gravity tugs on the eroded columns. The freezing and thawing of water in the columns' crevices expands and opens them wider, eventually breaking up the columns. Over the years, large chunks of rock have fallen off Mateo Teepee and crashed to its base. They can be seen today in the piles of natural debris that encircle the formation.

SLEEPING BEAR DUNE

LAKE MICHIGAN

A CHIPPEWA LEGEND

Sleeping Bear Dune is a large sand dune on a bluff overlooking Lake Michigan. The dune faces two small islands, South Manitou and North Manitou. At the beginning of the twentieth century, the dune was a round mound of sand completely covered by trees and shrubs. Behind it appeared a white, sand-covered hillside. The contrast between the dune and the hillside made the dune seem quite dark. From a passing canoe, this dark dune resembled a shaggy bear curled up in sleep. Over the years erosion has stripped away the dune's protective plant covering. Without the vegetation, the wind easily blows away sand and reshapes the mound.

Long ago in the land of the great northern forest, the hot sun beat down day after day. Little rain had fallen for many moons. The lush green forest had withered and turned brown. No plump berries clung to the bushes. No juicy grubs lived in the dry soil. There was nothing for Mother Bear and her two cubs to eat. So they wandered far and wide, searching for food.

One night a thunderstorm rumbled across the sky, but no rain fell. Instead, lightning leaped from the clouds and ignited a tree in the parched forest. The fire sprang to life, consuming trees and shrubs. It grew bigger and hotter, and soon it roared through the woodlands.

To escape the heat and flames, Mother Bear and her children plunged into the cool water of the Great Lake bordering the forest. Mother Bear saw that the land on the opposite shore was a luxuriant green. She knew she could find food and safety for her children there.

The bear family started to swim toward the distant shore. When they were halfway across the lake, a strong wind began to blow. The wind churned the water making the waves large and choppy. The swells turned into hills of water that crashed down upon the hapless bears. The cubs began to tire, but their mother urged them on.

Twelve miles from shore, one cub could go no further. Exhausted, it sank beneath the waves. The desperate mother bear tried to drag her remaining cub to safety. But she was weakened from many moons of scant food and could provide little help. Two miles from shore the second cub lost its strength. It, too, sank below the water.

Finally the mother bear reached land. She paced the shoreline for several days, calling out in vain to her children. Eventually she became so exhausted she lay down by the edge of the water and fell into a deep sleep.

The Great Spirit watched the mother bear with sadness. He admired her courage and perseverance, and he decided to reward her devotion toward her children. He raised the cubs slowly and changed them into beautiful green islands. Then he covered the mother with sand. The three bears remain there to this day as the Sleeping Bear Sand Dune and North and South Manitou Islands.

Sleeping Bear Dune and the Manitou Islands have their beginnings in the last ice age, which began about 75,000 years ago. Earth's climate began to chill. Large snowfalls blanketed the ground in central Canada and parts of northern Europe and Asia. In these regions the temperature never rose high enough to melt all the snow, not even in summer. Year after year fresh snow piled up on older snow. The tremendous weight of the snow compressed the lower layers into ice, which began to spread sideways. In this way gigantic ice sheets, called glaciers, formed. The glaciers began to grow in every direction and, pulled by gravity, they moved downhill.

An ice sheet two miles thick spread from Canada as far south as the present-day Ohio and Missouri river valleys. As the glacier flowed over the landscape, it plucked rocks and soil from the ground beneath it and incorporated them into the bottom of the ice. The debris ranged in size from tiny clay fragments to boulders as large as houses. The glacier held onto most of this rubble until the ice melted. Together, the ice and the debris reshaped the land by gouging, grinding, breaking, and polishing the rock that the glacier passed over. At the same time that the glacier wore away the terrain beneath it, it also pushed rock fragments in front of it. Like a bulldozer, the glacier scraped up loose material and piled it to the side.

Eventually the advance of the ice sheet was halted. Ice at the front of the glacier melted as fast as the ice sheet moved. The ice sheet could not cover new ground. It held its position for thousands of years. During this long "standstill," the glacier deposited tremendous amounts of sand, gravel, clay, and boulders at its edges. This jumble of debris formed large ridges known as moraines.

The end of the ice age came about 12,000 to 10,000 years ago when Earth's climate warmed. The melting ice sheets left behind the immense piles of rubble they had created. At this time the Great Lakes, including Lake Michigan, began to take shape. These lakes lie in river valleys that glaciers scoured and enlarged, and then blocked with moraines. The moraines prevent water from flowing away.

The tremendous weight of the glacier depressed the surface of the earth around the Great Lakes. After the ice melted, the surface slowly began to rise toward its previous elevation, a process that is still continuing today.

Sleeping Bear Dune on the shore of Lake Michigan lies on a moraine that forms the shoreline of Lake Michigan. The Manitou Islands are actually part of a submerged ridge of limestone that is covered with debris dumped by the glacier. Both islands have sand dunes.

During storms, powerful waves erode the shoreline, making loose sand available for dune development. But it is the action of strong winds that actually forms the dunes. Sand dunes take shape when wind deposits sand grains against a shrub, boulder, or other obstruction. The obstruction causes the sand to pile up into a mound. Sand dunes will shift and change shape unless they are anchored by a covering of plants whose roots hold the sand in place.

HORSESHOE FALLS AT NIAGARA FALLS

NIAGARA FALLS, CANADA

A SENECA LEGEND

Niagara Falls is the most famous waterfall in North America. Lying on the border of Ontario, Canada, and New York State, the falls attract millions of visitors each year. An island in the Niagara River splits the water flow into two parts just before the falls. The smaller flow plunges over the American Falls; the larger goes over Horseshoe Falls. At 180 feet, the American Falls is about 5 feet taller than Horseshoe Falls. However, Horseshoe Falls is about twice as wide as the American Falls.

Long ago a mighty Seneca tribe lived near the area now known as Niagara Falls. The members of the tribe took pride in the abundant crops they raised and in their prowess as bold and fearless hunters. But for several years a mysterious illness plagued the tribe, killing young and old. Life went on for the fortunate tribal members spared from death, but they remained ever watchful.

A beautiful maiden named Bending Willow was one who escaped this strange plague. Bending Willow was as graceful as reeds of grass swaying in the wind. Her laughter was as bubbly and refreshing as the brooks that tumbled through the forest. Many suitors vied for her favor, but she spurned them all. For Bending Willow's heart belonged to another, a handsome and skilled hunter from a distant tribe. She awaited the day that he would return and throw a red deer at her feet, a sign that he wanted her for his bride.

Among her suitors was a rich old chief called No Heart, who was as ugly as Bending Willow was beautiful. Chief No Heart's face was scarred and wrinkled like the gnarled bark of an ancient oak. His breath was foul, like the odor of rotting deer meat. The chief was as well-known for his cruelty as he was for his great wealth and his ugliness. When it came time to test the young men of his tribe to determine their worthiness as adult members of the community, No Heart devised tests of torture. These tests were much harsher than any tests of manhood the tribe had ever known.

One day, Chief No Heart announced his plans to marry Bending Willow. Fearing the chief's power and his thirst for vengeance, the parents of the girl dared not refuse. Bending Willow cried and pleaded with them to revoke their pledge. But they could not.

The night before her wedding, Bending Willow stole into the woods. Brokenhearted, she flung herself on the hard ground and cried until she had no more tears. In the distance she heard the roar of the great falls at Niagara. Suddenly, the sound of the crashing water gave her hope.

In the morning before anyone awoke, she crept back to her village and took her father's canoe. She set the craft in the water and paddled desperately toward the thundering falls. Preferring death to a marriage with Chief No Heart, she plunged over the falls. For an instant she saw only the bright green water below. Then to her astonishment she found herself floating on the great white wings of Hinu, the thunder god. The water parted before them and Bending Willow passed into a cave behind the falls.

Hinu wrapped the maiden in a warm blanket and placed her by a magic fire that burned beneath the falls. Its flames of red, green, yellow, and blue fused together to form a rainbow. After Bending Willow had rested, Hinu told her that he knew her sad story and invited her to stay with him until Chief No Heart died. Hinu also revealed that he kept careful watch over Bending Willow's tribe.

"A giant snake lies beneath your village," Hinu said. "He craves the taste of human blood and is not satisfied by the small number of people who die naturally. So he poisons the springs from which your people draw their water. That is why there is so much illness and death in your village. After the dead are buried, the snake drinks their blood. The taste of blood makes the snake even more ravenous. So when one death occurs, many more will follow until the snake is gorged. Then the snake sleeps for a while.

"When you return to your village," said Hinu, "convince your people to move near me. I will protect them from the giant snake."

Bending Willow stayed with Hinu a long time and learned many things. But her thoughts often strayed to the young man she loved. She wondered if she would ever see him again. Finally, Hinu learned of the death of the wicked chief and returned Bending Willow to her people. The maiden told her tribe all she knew about the great snake and persuaded them to move closer to Hinu's cave.

For many months the people enjoyed good health. But the greedy snake was not so easily deprived of his food. Eventually he discovered the new village and poisoned the water there. This angered Hinu. He grabbed a handful of the magic fire, molded it into thunderbolts, and flung them at the snake. The first thunderbolt stunned the snake, the second wounded it, and the third killed it.

The body of the snake stretched farther than the flight of twenty arrows. Hinu asked the people to push the dead snake into the river. It took the strength of all the men and women of the tribe to move the snake. At last, the snake drifted downstream. When it reached the edge of the falls, near the home of Hinu, the snake's head became wedged in the rocks. Its body coiled around itself and its great weight pressed down on the rocks, bending them into the shape of a drawn bow. Gradually the water washed away the snake, leaving behind the horseshoe-shaped falls we see today.

At long last the young hunter whom Bending Willow loved did return and carefully placed a red deer at her feet. They married and remained devoted to each other for the rest of their lives.

If you had a fish's view of a river, you would see that the river constantly plucks soil and rocks from the bottom and sides of its channel and sweeps them downstream. You would notice that the pebbles, rocks, and other heavy sediments roll, slide, or bump along the river bottom. The sediments collide with each other and with the rocks lining the channel. Like tools for cutting and grinding, the sediments scour and chip the riverbed, making it wider and deeper.

This kind of erosion can give birth to waterfalls. When a river flows from a bed of hard rock to one of soft rock, it wears away the soft rock faster and deeper than the hard rock. In time a steep cliff develops where the streambed changes from hard to soft rock. When the water plunges over the cliff it creates a waterfall. This process formed Niagara Falls. The falls are located on the 35-mile-long Niagara River, which connects Lake Erie with Lake Ontario.

The erosion, however, does not stop. The falling water creates a whirlpool at the base of the falls. The whirlpool eats away the bottom of the cliff. Eventually undermined, the top breaks off bit by bit and the position of the waterfall moves slowly upstream.

Niagara Falls formed about 10,000 years ago at the end of the last ice age. Since that time the falls have receded nearly 7 miles upriver. In the nineteenth century the falls eroded at a rate of 5.5 feet per year. Since then some of the water has been diverted from the falls to power plants to use in generating electricity. The erosion rate has decreased to less than 1 foot a year. Nevertheless, Niagara Falls is expected to disappear into Lake Erie in about 23,000 years.

The name Niagara comes from the word *Nee-ah-ga-rah* in the Seneca language. It means "thundering waters." The Seneca people believed that a powerful spirit lived within the waters of the falls. Each year they offered a human sacrifice to appease the spirit. A young woman was placed in a canoe laden with fruits and flowers, and sent to her death over the falls.

MARTHA'S VINEYARD AND NANTUCKET ISLAND

OFF THE COAST OF MASSACHUSETTS

A WAMPANOAG LEGEND

Every summer tens of thousands of tourists flock to the islands of Martha's Vineyard and Nantucket off the coast of Massachusetts. They are drawn to the islands' sandy beaches, numerous inlets and ponds, and mild climate. When English explorers first came to the islands they found a well-developed society of native people, the Wampanoags. The Wampanoags raised corn, beans, pumpkins, and other crops. They harvested whales and large fish from the sea, and were skilled artisans in wood, leather, and stone. But the Wampanoags had little natural immunity against the diseases the English settlers transmitted. As a result, epidemics nearly wiped out their population.

Long ago the mighty giant Maushop dwelled on the island of Martha's Vineyard. He towered over the tallest of trees and satisfied his hunger by harvesting whales and large fish from the sea. Maushop cooked his catch on the windswept cliffs now known as Gay Head. The immense heat of his cooking fires, along with the blood and grease from the whales, burned and stained the ground. The drab coloring of the clay turned to beautiful shades of red, blue, yellow, and green. To fuel his cooking fires Maushop uprooted large trees, which is why nothing larger than a shrub grows on Gay Head to this day. When he finished eating, the giant left the remains on the cliffs, where the fossilized bones of whales and fish can still be found.

Maushop was as wise and generous as he was strong and tall. He shared his catch of whales and great fish with the local people. In return the grateful people provided Maushop with tobacco for his pipe.

In times of trouble, the people came to him for advice. One day a young woman and a young man sought Maushop's counsel. The two wished to marry but the man owned little land. The woman's father would not permit the union until the young man possessed an entire island. The father was a wealthy chief with many grapevines, and an abundance of ponds stocked with clams, oysters, crabs, perch, ducks, and geese. His vast holdings also included swamps rich in cranberries, and fields well-suited for growing corn and other food crops. He wanted his daughter to marry a rich man, not a man who lived in poverty.

After the lovers told the giant their sad story, Maushop advised them to return to their separate tribes. Disappointed, the lovers did as they were told, certain that the giant would be of no help. Meanwhile, Maushop began to fill his pipe with tobacco. Because the pipe was so large, he needed many, many bales of tobacco to fill it. When it was full, Maushop lit the pipe with a bolt of lightning and sat down to smoke. Afterward, the giant waded out to sea. There, he emptied the ashes from his pipe.

The embers hissed and roared. Lightning flashed and thunder boomed. A great cloud of steam billowed into the air, creating a dense fog that stretched for miles. When the fog cleared, a new island could be seen. Thus the island of Nantucket arose from the ashes of Maushop's pipe.

The giant returned to the young lovers and hoisted the man on his back and placed the woman in the crook of his arm. In this fashion, he carried them to the new island. Maushop then returned to the young woman's tribe, snatched her father off the ground, and brought him to Nantucket. This angered the father and he protested loudly.

On the island, the lovers greeted the old man. When he learned that the island belonged to the young man, the father calmed down and gave his blessing for the marriage.

As there was no longer any reason to delay the wedding, Maushop immediately conducted the ceremony. The husband and wife lived on Nantucket for the rest of their lives, as did their children and grandchildren and those who came after them.

When the European settlers came to America, Maushop realized there would be no place for him on Martha's Vineyard. So he retired in disgust. But to this day you can still detect his presence. Every time Maushop lights up his pipe, a fog rolls in from off the coast.

Cape Cod, a sandy peninsula in New England, looks like a hook when seen from the air. The Cape juts out about 25 miles eastward from the Massachusetts mainland and then continues for about 30 miles in a northerly direction. To the south of the Cape lie the islands of Martha's Vineyard, Nantucket, Block Island, and Long Island. During the last ice age, which began about 75,000 years ago and ended about 10,000 years ago, the ice sheets in Canada, Northern Europe, and Asia enlarged. Inch by inch they pushed southward, claiming vast amounts of territory. As the ice sheets expanded they locked up more and more of Earth's water by turning it to ice. Slowly the level of the ocean began to fall. This plunge in sea level exposed more land along the coasts than is visible today. As a result, the New England coastline extended about 100 miles outward from its present position. The newly uncovered land formed a coastal plain of low hills and flat land that gradually sloped toward the coast.

The glacier responsible for the formation of Cape Cod and the islands originated in the highlands of Labrador, Canada. As it grew, the ice sheet advanced southward, covering eastern

Canada. About 25,000 years ago it crossed into New England and spread as far south as present-day New York City and Long Island. The glacier continued to thicken. It entombed what is now Cape Cod and the islands in an ice layer 1,500 feet deep. Ice this thick would cover the Empire State Building with an extra 250 feet to spare! In New Hampshire the ice grew even thicker, covering the White Mountains. When the glacier reached the sea, large blocks broke off in the water and drifted away as icebergs.

Like the glacier responsible for fashioning Lake Michigan, this ice sheet swept away everything in its path. It, too, wore away the terrain beneath it and pushed rubble to the front and sides. When this ice sheet finally halted, it held its position for 7,000 years, depositing vast amounts of sand, rock, and other debris along its edges. These deposits piled up into mighty ridges that later became the islands of Martha's Vineyard, Nantucket, Block Island, and Long Island.

When the standstill ended, the glacier began its "retreat." More ice melted from the front of it than could be replaced by the glacier's forward motion. The glacier came to another standstill that lasted for thousands of years more, forming another immense ridge from its rubble. This second ridge created Cape Cod.

Finally, about 13,000 years ago, the climate began to warm and the glaciers began to thaw. Gradually the sea level rose. Over the course of seven thousand years or so, the ocean level rose about 400 feet, flooding the "new" coastal plain. Only the highest hills and ridges remained above the surface of the ocean. These high places included Cape Cod and the islands. Although ice originally formed these landscapes, wind, waves, and living things are constantly changing them.

HALF DOME AND NORTH DOME

YOSEMITE NATIONAL PARK, CALIFORNIA

A MIWOK LEGEND

Yosemite Valley is in the heart of the Sierra Nevada Mountains, about
200 miles east of San Francisco. In Yosemite, granite cliffs soar more than
half a mile above the valley floor. Some of the highest waterfalls in the world
cascade over these cliffs. The Southern Miwok tribes lived in Yosemite
for more than 2,000 years. They called the valley Ah-wah'-nee, which
means "deep, grassy valley." The name Yosemite is a corruption of the
Miwok word, uzaumati, which means "grizzly bear."

Long ago Tis-sa-ack and her husband, Nangas, left their home in the arid plains to find a better place to start a family. On his back, Nangas carried a light roll of deer skins. In his hand, he held a walking stick. Tis-sa-ack bore a heavy, cone-shaped basket on her back. In her arms she clutched a cradle that she hoped would hold a baby one day.

The couple crossed the plains and climbed the high mountains that loomed before them. For many days they traversed the rugged slopes. Footsore and weary, they passed through quiet meadows and pleasant valleys but did not stop. They pressed on and on searching for a place more to their liking. Finally, from a peak high in the mountains they looked down upon Ah-wah'-nee, the Yosemite Valley. They saw a sparkling blue lake and a land lush with grass, trees, and shrubs. They knew instantly that this beautiful place would be their new home.

Thirsty from their long journey, the couple rushed toward the valley and its inviting lake. Tis-sa-ack reached the water first. So great was her thirst that she filled the basket and drank from it many times without stopping. In her greed, she drank so much that by the time Nangas reached the shore, the lake was dry. Not even a basketful of water remained.

Enraged and choking with thirst, Nangas began to beat his wife with his walking stick. Tis-sa-ack fled, leaving the baby cradle behind. Nangas followed, striking his wife again and again. Weeping, Tis-sa-ack ran faster. But Nangas continued to beat her. Terrified, Tis-sa-ack turned and flung the basket at him.

The Great Spirit witnessed their quarrel. Angered that the greedy and violent humans had shattered the peace of his beautiful valley, he punished them. The moment that Tis-sa-ack turned to face her husband, the Great Spirit transformed them both into large stone domes. Nangas became North Dome. Tis-sa-ack became Half Dome. The deep lines that trail down Half Dome's steep cliff are Tis-sa-ack's tears. As for the conical basket, it too turned to stone and became Basket Dome at the foot of North Dome. And the forgotten baby cradle? The Great Spirit transformed it into the Royal Arches.

Five hundred million years ago, a vast sea covered the area where Yosemite now lies. Mud, sand, and other sediments settled on the sea floor. At first the sediments fit together loosely. Gradually, more and more sediments fell on top of them, creating new layers. The weight of the overlying layers slowly pressed the underlying particles tightly together. Eventually the sediments hardened and changed into sedimentary rock.

Starting about 200 million years ago, immense forces within the earth's crust squeezed the sedimentary rock layers. The rock began to fold and rise above sea level. What was once seafloor now began to take the shape of mountains.

Hot molten rock called magma collected beneath the new mountain range, pushing the mountains even higher. The magma cooled and hardened into granite, forming the core of the Sierra Nevada Mountains.

About 60 to 80 million years ago, the Sierra Nevada stopped rising. The forces that wear away the earth's surface—wind, rain, ice, flowing water, and gravity—were already at work stripping off the sedimentary rock layers. By 10 to 20 million years ago, most of these rock layers had disappeared, exposing the granite core. The landscape became one of rolling hills, wide valleys, and gentle, winding streams.

Renewed uplift started 5 to 10 million years ago. Earthquakes drove the granite upward and tilted it. The tilting made the western slopes of the mountains much steeper than the eastern slopes. This increased steepness made the streams flow faster and erode the valleys more deeply. The Merced River cascaded through what is now Yosemite Valley, carving a steep gorge.

Then, 3 million years ago a series of ice ages began. In the high peaks surrounding Yosemite long and thick rivers of ice called valley glaciers took shape. Pulled by gravity, these glaciers inched forward. The glaciers expanded and advanced into the stream valleys, picking up rocks in their path. Embedded in the ice, these rocks scraped and gouged the land.

Over time more glaciers entered Yosemite and sheared off the lower sides of the gorge. This transformed the narrow, V-shaped gorge into a broad, U-shaped valley. Some streams entering the valley were cut off by the grinding walls of ice. When the glacier finally melted, these streams were left "hanging" above the valley floor, creating magnificent waterfalls.

North Dome, Basket Dome, and Royal Arches were all overrun and sculpted by glaciers, leaving them with jagged edges. After the ice melted, weathering and exfoliation rounded off the sharp corners of these formations. During exfoliation the outer layers of rock wear off, like the layers of an onion, giving it a rounded shape.

Exfoliation can also cause gigantic slabs of granite to break off from mountain peaks. This is how Half Dome, the most prominent peak in Yosemite, got its distinctive shape. Half Dome looks as if a giant hand sliced it in half. Exfoliation shaped Half Dome long before the Ice Age without any help from glaciers.

MOUNT ST. HELENS AND THE COLUMBIA CASCADES

WASHINGTON STATE

A KLICKITAT LEGEND

Mount St. Helens in southwestern Washington State was once known for its beautiful snow-capped peak, sparkling streams, and scenic lookouts. Silent for 123 years, the volcano awakened in March 1980, puffing steam, ash, and gas from a summit vent. Two months later, Mount St. Helens exploded, blowing out its northern flank in the largest landslide ever witnessed in human history. While the eruption surprised most Americans, the Native American tribes of Washington and Oregon had long known of the explosive nature of the volcanoes in the region. The Klickitat people call Mount St. Helens Tah-one-lat-clah, or "Fire Mountain."

When the earth was young, Tyhee Saghalie, chief of the gods, lived with his two sons. Together the father and sons traveled down Great River, which is now called the Columbia. They came to where the Bonneville Dam is today. Both sons saw the beauty of the land and each wanted it for himself. So, as siblings do today, they quarreled.

To stop the argument, Saghalie took his bow and shot two arrows, one to the north and another to the west. Then he said to his sons, "Follow the arrows and make your homes where they have fallen."

One son journeyed northward and became the father of the Klickitat people. The other settled in the West and fathered the Multnomah people. To keep peace, Saghalie separated the two tribes by placing between them the huge Cascade mountain range. The mountains looked the way they do today, except there were no large, snow-covered peaks. The Great River flowed broad and deep between the mountains, a sign of peace. Saghalie built an immense stone bridge across the river so the tribes could maintain a friendship. Saghalie called the bridge *Tomanowas* or "peace bridge."

For many years the Klickitats and the Multnomahs remained friends. They sat side by side at each other's campfires and recounted the famous deeds of their ancestors. On special occasions they feasted and danced together. They not only shared good times, but came together in times of sorrow, too. When a soul departed from one tribe, the other tribe joined in the funeral chants.

But then one day the people grew selfish and greedy. They no longer shared their joys, or supported each other in times of grief. The two tribes forgot their tradition of friendship and made war upon each other.

This angered Saghalie. In his wrath he stopped the sun from shining. Soon, cold and snow descended upon the people. They searched for fire with which to warm themselves, but they found none.

In all the world only Loowit still had fire. She was an old, wrinkled woman who had kept herself from wrongdoing. When the people discovered Loowit's fire they tried to steal it. But Loowit, old and stooped as she was, could outrun them. Her pursuers were so stiff with cold they could not run fast enough.

Loowit saw the misery of the people and wanted to share her fire with them. She begged permission to do so from Saghalie and he granted her wish. Loowit kindled a fire on the bridge and the people came to share it.

With the acquisition of fire, life improved for all the tribes. No longer consumed with the need to keep warm, the people found time to build bigger lodges, sew better clothes, and prepare more interesting foods to eat. Loowit's gift of fire gave the tribes the gift of peace and prosperity.

Loowit's kindness pleased Saghalie and he promised to grant her any wish. The old woman desired eternal youth and beauty, so Saghalie changed her into a beautiful young maiden. As might be expected, many chiefs came to the bridge and fell in love with beautiful Loowit. For a long time Loowit paid them no heed, until finally one day two chiefs stirred her heart. One was Klickitat from the North and the other was Wiyeast from the West. Both chiefs wanted her so much that they fought each other for her love.

Loowit did not want to choose between the chiefs. So they waged bigger and bigger battles as they attempted to win her affection. Their warriors joined the quarrel, too. Soon much blood was spilled, the land was ravaged, and all the new lodges were destroyed.

Saghalie became angry with the chiefs for constantly fighting. He became angry with Loowit for refusing to make a choice. In his anger, he destroyed the stone bridge because the great river was no longer a sign of peace. Huge rocks tumbled into the river. They remain there to this day near the Bonneville Dam.

Saghalie's rage was not spent. He covered each of the three young people with stone and turned them into separate mountains. Klickitat became Mount Adams, and Wiyeast became Mount Hood. Loowit resides inside Mount St. Helens. Most of the time she sleeps quietly, but every hundred years or so, something disturbs her rest. Then she awakens and blows the top off the mountain.

Much geologic evidence supports the Klickitat legend that a land bridge once spanned the Columbia River. Near Bonneville, the majestic cliffs lining the Columbia Gorge are steep and unstable. Landslides are common. About 500 years ago a powerful earthquake weakened Table Mountain, which stood about 3 miles north of the gorge. The mountain gave way, triggering a series of landslides that engulfed 15 square miles of the Columbia Gorge.

The debris formed a massive dam more than a mile wide and 200 feet high. This dam blocked the flow of the river for a few months and created a lake that extended nearly 70 miles upriver. During this time the Klickitats could have easily walked across the debris dam.

The water behind the dam grew higher and higher until it finally washed over the top. As the water overtopped the dam, it cut downward through the debris. The dam collapsed and the impounded water escaped in a monumental flood.

The river's flow returned to normal except that its channel had shifted a mile to the south. All that remained of the dam were enormous slabs of rock that created magnificent rapids—the Columbia Cascades. In 1938 the rapids vanished when water backed up by the newly constructed Bonneville Dam covered them.

Mount St. Helens has come to symbolize the deadly, unpredictable nature of volcanoes. In the spring of 1980, when Mount St. Helens began to stir after more than a century of silence, geologists rushed to observe it. For two months they scrutinized the volcano's every change, including its earthquakes, gas emissions, and surface changes. Yet none anticipated the events of May 18, when a large earthquake shook the mountain. A bulge on the north face broke loose in a colossal landslide. From within the mountain, steam, ash, and rocks exploded out sideways, reaching speeds of more than 600 miles per hour. The blast leveled everything for miles around.

Meanwhile, the landslide debris rampaged down the mountain's slopes. Some of it poured into Spirit Lake, filling half the lake. Some charged into the Toutle River, causing it to overflow its banks. This debris avalanche ripped trees from their roots and swept away roads, bridges, and houses. It filled the river valley with a layer of debris 150 feet thick.

After the initial explosion, Mount St. Helens erupted upward. A giant plume of rock and ash shot up more than 12 miles high and formed a dark cloud that filled the sky. Rocks and ash pelted the countryside below. The eruption continued for nine hours. Winds carried the ash northeastward. It fell from the sky and covered eastern Washington with a gritty gray coating.

Mount St. Helens has quieted considerably since 1980, erupting every so often with a relatively minor explosion. But scientists know that someday the volcano will blow its top again.

MOUNT SHASTA

NORTHERN CALIFORNIA

A MODOC LEGEND

Mount Shasta is a massive, snow-clad volcano, 14,161 feet high. It is located in northern California, 40 miles south of the Oregon border. Like Mount St. Helens in the years before its 1980 eruption, Mount Shasta draws hikers, fishers, and campers to its wilderness. A resort that opened on Mount Shasta in 1985 caters to downhill skiers. Over the past 4,500 years Mount Shasta has erupted an average of once every 600 years. The last eruption took place about 200 years ago. In the early 1980s minor earthquakes jiggled the mountain. Volcanologists predicted that future eruptions of this "sleeping giant" are quite likely.

Long ago when the earth was young, Sky Spirit grew weary of his home in the Above-World because it was too cold. So with a large stone, he carved a hole in the sky and pushed snow and ice through it. The snow and ice tumbled downward until they finally reached the surface of the earth and began to pile up in a mound. The mound of ice and snow rose higher and higher until it formed a mountain that nearly touched the sky. Today, this mountain is called Mount Shasta.

Sky Spirit then climbed through the hole he had made and stepped from cloud to cloud until he reached the mountaintop. From there he descended Mt. Shasta. Halfway down, he decided that the mountain needed trees. From that point on, wherever he jabbed his finger into the ground, a tree sprouted. The snow melted in his footsteps and the meltwater ran down the mountain, making the rivers and providing moisture for the trees to grow. Sky Spirit collected the leaves that fell from the trees. He blew on them and the leaves turned into birds.

Next, Sky Spirit took a stick that he had carried from the sky and broke the small end into many pieces. He threw the pieces into the river. The big fragments became otters and beavers. The little fragments became fish. From the middle of the stick Sky Spirit formed all the other animals except the grizzly bear.

He saved the big end of the stick to create the grizzly. And when he saw his creations, he appointed the grizzly master of all the other animals. For in that time, the grizzlies were stronger and more cunning than grizzlies are today. They walked upon two feet and could speak. But their shaggy fur and their sharp claws made them look so ferocious that the Sky Spirit banished them to the forest at the foot of the mountain.

When Sky Spirit was done, he liked what he saw and decided to make his lodge on Earth. He hollowed out Mt. Shasta and brought his wife and little red-haired daughter to join him. In the center of their new lodge, Sky Spirit built a fire. He made a hole in the top of the mountain so the smoke could escape. Sometimes when he threw a log on the fire, sparks would fly from the smoke hole and the earth would tremble.

One night as Sky Spirit and his family sat around the fire, a great storm arose. The wind howled with such savage fury that the mountain shook and the smoke blew back into the lodge. Annoyed, Sky Spirit sent his daughter to the smoke hole to tell the wind to blow more gently. He warned his daughter not to poke her head outside because the wind might catch her in its embrace and blow her away. "Just put your arm out to get wind's attention, then talk to him," he said.

The little girl hurried to the smoke hole and thrust her arm through the hole. But she wanted to see the ocean where the wind was born, so she put her head out, too. The wind caught the little girl by her long red hair and whirled her out of the lodge. Down the mountainside she flew, over the snow and ice. She landed at the edge of the great forest. There, Father Grizzly found her cold, bruised, and shivering with fright. He carried the little girl home to his wife, who warmed her by the fire, treated her injuries, and gave her food to eat. Mother Grizzly brought up the little girl with her family of cubs.

When the little girl was grown, she married the eldest son of the grizzlies. They were happy together and had many children. The children, being half Spirit and half Grizzly, had much less hair than grizzly bears, but they didn't quite look like spirits either. They were the first people. All the grizzlies were proud of this new race of creatures, so they built a lodge for the red-headed spirit woman and her children near Mount Shasta. It is called Little Mount Shasta.

When Mother Bear neared the end of her life, she worried that she had been wrong in keeping the red-headed girl and not returning her to her father. So she sent her eldest grandson to the top of Mount Shasta to tell the Sky Spirit where he could find his long-lost daughter.

When he heard the news, Sky Spirit raced down the mountain in great haste. The grizzlies stood in front of the new lodge waiting to greet Sky Spirit. They thought he would be overjoyed to be reunited with his daughter.

But Sky Spirit expected his daughter to look exactly as she had the last time he saw her—as a small child. When he saw that she was fully grown and the wife of a grizzly and the mother of a new race of strange creatures, he became enraged. One of his laws had been broken. For he had said in the beginning that only those of the same kind could have children together.

Sky Spirit cursed the grizzlies. "You will never speak again. You will use your hands as feet and walk on all four legs. You will look downward. Only when you face danger can you stand erect."

Sky Spirit led his daughter to his mountaintop lodge, where he put out its fire forever. Then, stepping from cloud to cloud, he guided his daughter back to their old lodge in the sky. Abandoned, his grandchildren wandered all over the earth and became the ancestors of all the people now living. When a child is born, it remembers how it was deserted in the beginning and so it cries.

The story of Mount Shasta's formation is closely linked to the theory of plate tectonics. According to the theory of plate tectonics, Earth's solid outer shell (the crust) is broken up into a number of large pieces called plates. The plates fit snugly together like the pieces of a cracked eggshell. The plates float in different directions atop a layer of partially melted rock. As they float the plates carry the continents and oceans on top of them.

Most of the boundaries between plates are sharply defined cracks called faults. There are three main kinds of plate boundaries—transform, divergent, and convergent. At transform boundaries, plates grind past each other, often triggering earthquakes.

Divergent boundaries form where plates pull apart. Molten rock gurgles up between the separating plates, forming new crust and pushing the plates farther apart.

Convergent boundaries occur where plates collide. When two plates carrying continents crash together, their edges squeeze each other like a giant trash compactor, folding the land and pushing it upward. Magnificent mountain ranges result.

But, if a plate carrying the ocean floor collides with a plate carrying a continent, the ocean floor is pushed beneath the continent, and eventually melts. Part of the melting plate joins with the molten rock beneath the crust. The rest collects as magma below the surface of the overriding continent. This magma slowly raises the land above it, creating mountains.

In some places the rising magma bursts through to the surface of the overriding continent and forms a chain of volcanoes. This has been happening in the Pacific Northwest for nearly one million years. There, a part of the Pacific Ocean floor is being pushed beneath the North American continent. The resulting magma has built up the Cascade Range, a string of explosive volcanoes that extends from Mount Garibaldi in Canada to Lassen Peak in northern California. The magma fuels Mount Shasta, Mount St. Helens, and the other volcanoes in the region.

THE HAWAIIAN ISLANDS

PELE, THE HAWAIIAN GODDESS OF FIRE

AN AUKELENUIAIKU LEGEND

The Big Island of Hawaii is a land where new earth is born. Here volcanoes rumble and steam, shoot lava high into the air, or release it quietly from cracks on their flanks. From the top of its highest mountain, 13,796 feet above sea level, to its base on the ocean floor 18,000 feet below sea level, the Big Island is completely volcanic in origin. Five overlapping volcanoes make up the formation. The Big Island is just one in a chain of volcanic islands that stretches 1,500 miles across the central Pacific from the Big Island to Midway Island.

Pele was a beautiful Hawaiian goddess. When she took human form, she was more beautiful than the loveliest woman that had ever walked the earth. Pele's eyes sparkled with a piercing brilliance, and her long, silky hair shone red in their glow. But Pele had a temper. When she became angry, she let loose a flood of lava that covered the ground, incinerating everything in its path. For beautiful Pele was the fire goddess and she possessed a magic shovel. Wherever she struck the earth with her magic shovel, she created a pit in which volcanic fires burned.

Pele grew up on an island far to the south of Hawaii. There she lived in peace and harmony with her many brothers and sisters until a sorcerer came into their lives. Pele's older sister Na-maka-o-ka-hai, the goddess of the sea, fell in love with the sorcerer, and the two married.

After a time, however, the sorcerer took note of Pele's great beauty. At the same time, Pele took note of him. Although they both knew they were doing something wrong, they secretly married. They hoped they could keep their relationship secret from Na-maka-o-ka-hai.

The sorcerer had tremendous powers. He could soar through the air like a bird, swim across the sea like a fish, and run over the earth like the wind. With magic he defeated his enemies and brought his dead brothers back to life. Yet despite his great powers, the sorcerer could not prevent Na-maka-o-ka-hai from discovering the truth. When she learned of the betrayal, Na-maka-o-ka-hai became enraged and vowed to kill Pele. In her wrath, Na-maka-o-ka-hai created high tides and flooding sea waters to destroy Pele's home.

The sorcerer's powers were no match for Na-maka-o-ka-hai's. He could not protect Pele. So the rest of Pele's family came to her aid. Together they tried to stop Na-maka-o-ka-hai, but to no avail. Na-maka-o-ka-hai destroyed their homes, too, and forced Pele and the others to flee the island.

Pele headed north to the Hawaiian Islands in a great canoe, accompanied by her little sister and her brothers. Her brothers—the gods of wind, current, and tide—swept the craft along. Eventually Pele landed on Niihau, the island of the fire-thrower goddess. Pele was warmly welcomed there and handsomely entertained.

By and by, Pele grew restless and left in search of a new home. Soon she reached the island of Kauai. There she used her magic shovel to dig a pit deep enough to house her whole family. As she dug, she opened an immense crater in the earth. Molten rock spilled from the hole, and volcanic smoke rose high in the sky.

Na-maka-o-ka-hai, still bent on vengeance, searched for signs of Pele. From the highest point in all the lands, she looked upon the seas. When she spied the smoke rising above Kauai, she rushed to the island and tried once more to kill Pele. In fierce fighting, Na-maka-o-ka-hai injured Pele and left her for dead.

But Pele survived and fled with her family to the island of Oahu. Near what is now the city of Honolulu, Pele dug another fire pit. Here, however, she struck water, which filled the crater and drowned her fires. Then Pele moved to another location on Oahu, a site known today as Diamond Head. Again, she dug a fire pit, but again water streamed into the crater, extinguishing the flames.

With her family, Pele moved from island to island along the Hawaiian chain, seeking a new home. Each time she dug a fire pit, water quenched its flames. Finally she arrived at the island of Maui. On the high mountain called Haleakala, Pele dug with her magic shovel. Down, down, down she dug, throwing out vast amounts of lava. This time no water seeped in, and Pele and her family settled in their new home.

From her high perch, Na-maka-o-ka-hai spotted the volcanic smoke and saw that her sister still lived. Once more she pursued Pele and confronted the fire goddess in her new home. In anger and fear, Pele shook the earth and threw great fountains of lava into the air. Na-maka-o-ka-hai caused the seas to rage and the waves to batter the land. For many days the sisters fought. Although Pele put up a valiant struggle, she could not defeat Na-maka-o-ka-hai. Na-maka-o-ka-hai tore Pele apart and heaped the fragments of her bones on a hill. The hill still stands today. It is called *Ka-iwi-o-Pele*—the bones of Pele.

Na-maka-o-ka-hai returned to her home, jubilant in victory. Pele's other siblings, believing the fire goddess to be dead, mourned her greatly. Unbeknownst to anyone, however, Pele's spirit had taken flight.

Pele's spirit settled on the Big Island of Hawaii where she first made her home in Mauna Loa volcano. Soon afterward, Na-maka-o-ka-hai noticed volcanic smoke wafting upward from Mauna Loa. Inside it she saw Pele's spirit form and realized that she could never defeat it. Thus she descended from her mountain watch and let her sister be.

Pele dug her final home in the caldera of Kilauea's volcano. The remainder of Pele's family joined her there. They serve her to this day by caring for her volcanic fires and pouring out rivers of lava at her command. At times Pele loses her patience with her brothers and sisters. Then she stomps the floor of the fire pit, setting off an earthquake. Sometimes Pele becomes so angry, she destroys the beautiful valleys that her siblings enjoy by sending a river of lava careening over the land.

The Hawaiian Islands are the tops of huge volcanoes that rise from the Pacific Ocean floor and poke high above the surface of the sea. Through their Pele myths the ancient Hawaiians clearly demonstrated their awareness of the geologic history of their home.

According to the ancient Hawaiians, Pele progressed from Niihau to Kauai, Oahu, Maui, and then to the Big Island, from northwest to southeast. The order of Pele's flight accurately reflects the age progression from oldest to youngest island in the Hawaiian chain. The southernmost island—the Big Island—is the youngest one. Two of the world's most active volcanoes, Kilauea and Mauna Loa, continue to build it up.

The Pele myths also recognize that volcanoes die out as islands age. Maui, the second-youngest island, last erupted around 1790 and is in its final stages of volcanic activity. In the not-too-distant future its volcanic flame will die out. Farther to the north, the volcanoes of Oahu, Kauai, Niihau, and the rest of the islands are all extinct.

Finally the myths show that battering sea waves wear away the islands. The amount of erosion is progressively greater moving southeast to northwest—again from youngest to oldest islands. The sea, however, is not alone in its destruction. Wind, rain, and running water strip the islands' soil and level the peaks of the extinct volcanoes.

Most volcanoes, such as Mount St. Helens and Mount Shasta, lie on the edge of tectonic plates. The Hawaiian Islands are an exception. They sit in the middle of the Pacific plate far from any plate boundaries. The key to their existence rests far below the Big Island. There, anchored in Earth's mantle layer is a tremendous heat source. This "hot spot" produces a magma plume, a narrow column of magma that moves up a deep fault toward the surface. Like a blowtorch, the plume melts through the underside of the plate above it, creating volcanoes on the surface.

On the ocean floor, enough molten rock may pour out to form an island. The hot spot will feed the volcano until the shifting plate eventually carries the island away from its magma source. Then a new volcano will form over the plume. As the other Hawaiian volcanoes drifted away from the hot spot they were cut off from the magma source and their volcanoes became extinct.

The Pacific plate creeps northward at a rate of 3 to 5 inches a year. Right now the part of the plate carrying the Big Island of Hawaii (the youngest island) overlies the hot spot. The hot spot may be 200 miles across, with narrow vertical "pipes" that feed individual volcanoes.

Magma from this hot spot fuels Kilauea and Mauna Loa volcanoes. It has also created a new volcano, Loihi, about 20 miles south of the Big Island. Loihi rises more than 10,000 feet above the ocean floor but is still 3,000 feet shy of breaking through the water. If Loihi keeps growing it will form a new Hawaiian island in approximately 20,000 years.

SOURCE NOTES

[1] The legend of the Hot Springs of Arkansas was adapted from two legends, "The Legend of Hot Springs" and "The Great Spirit and the Dragon," which appeared in *Folklore of Romantic Arkansas, vol. 1,* by Fred W. Allsop, published by The Grolier Society in 1931. According to Allsop, he adapted his version from one recorded by J.W. Buell in *Legends of the Ozarks* in 1880.

[2] The legend of the Grand Canyon was adapted from a version recorded by explorer John Wesley Powell in his *Manuscripts of the Numic Peoples of the Western North America, 1868–1880.*

[3] The legend of Manitou Springs was adapted mainly from the version told by George F. Ruxton in *Adventures in Mexico and the Rocky Mountains,* published in 1848.

[4] The first printed version of the Hell's Canyon legend was recorded by Madge Maynard in the *Oregon Teachers Monthly* in May 1905. Ella E. Clark expanded on it in her book, *Indian Legends of the Pacific Northwest,* in 1953. According to Ella Clark, this legend was corroborated and elaborated upon by Caleb Whitman of the Nez Percé tribe on the Umatilla Reservation in August 1950.

[5] The myth of the Black Hills is a retelling of a Lakota legend recorded by James LaPointe, an Oglala Lakota Sioux elder, in his book, *Legends of the Lakota,* published in 1976.

[6] The legend of the Badlands was adapted from one told by Red Bird, a member of the Yankton division of the Sioux confederation, and a historian of his tribe. The legend, published after Red Bird's death, appeared in the *Indian School Journal,* published by the Chilocco Indian School in Oklahoma in 1937.

[7] The Mateo Teepee myth is a retelling of a Cheyenne legend recorded by Ella E. Clark in *Indian Legends from the Northern Rockies,* published in 1966.

[8] This telling of the Sleeping Bear Dune legend was adapted primarily from "Indian Legends of Northern Michigan," by John C. Wright, published in *Michigan History Magazine*, volume 2 (January 1918), and from "Historical Notes," *Michigan History Magazine*, volume 10 (July 1926). Neither source gave attribution to the original Native American storytellers.

[9] The telling of the origin of Horseshoe Falls is based on "A Seneca Legend of Hi-nu and Niagara" by Erminnie A. Smith in *Myths of the Iroquois* published in 1883. It was also influenced by "The Bended Rocks: A Story of Niagara" written by Margaret Compton in her book *Snow Bird and the Water Tiger and Other American Indian Tales,* published in 1895.

[10] The legend of the origin of Nantucket was adapted from one recorded by Dr. William Baylies sometime between 1786 and 1793, and a similar one contributed by an anonymous author about the same time. Neither writer attributed the legend to a specific Wampanoag storyteller.

[11] The Yosemite legend was adapted from several sources, including the "Legend of Tis-se'-yak" found in Katharine Berry Judson's *Myths and Legends of California and the Old Southwest*, published in 1912. None of the sources credited the original Miwok storytellers.

[12] This adaptation of the Mt. St. Helens and Columbia Cascades legend was influenced by several different versions, including one by Katharine Judson in her book, *Myths and Legends of the Pacific Northwest: Especially of Washington and Oregon*, published in 1910.

[13] The Mount Shasta legend was based mainly on a Modoc legend recorded by Joaquin Miller during the 1850s and retold by Ella Clark in her book, *Indian Legends of the Pacific Northwest.* It was also influenced by a Shasta legend found in *American Myths & Legends, Volume II* by Charles M. Skinner. A Shasta woman named Mattie, who died in 1878, had told the legend to Skinner.

[14] The legend of the Hawaiian Islands was adapted from one recorded by William D. Westervelt in *Hawaiian Legends of Volcanoes*, published in 1916, and a similar one contributed by Martha Warren Beckwith in *Hawaiian Mythology*, published in 1940. Neither author attributes the legend to a specific source.

INDEX